Filling in the Gaps

Finding Pre-1865 Ships Passenger Lists to Canada

By

Lorine McGinnis Schulze

© 2014 Lorine McGinnis Schulze

All Rights Reserved

Cover Image © AlienCat fotolia.com

ISBN-13:
978-1505397628

ISBN-10:
1505397626

Table of Contents

Where Are the Ships Passenger Lists for Canada Before 1865? 6

How Can I Find My Ancestor's Year of Immigration? 7

1801 A List of Names Going Through to Upper Canada From New Brunswick 8

Passengers from Lachine to Selkirk's Baldoon Settlement Kent County, Ontario 1804 10

List of Baldoon Settlers and their children, 1809 14

Passengers from Lachine to Selkirk's Baldoon Settlement in Kent County, Ontario 1812 18

New Brunswick Passenger Lists 1815-1838 21

Settlers intending to emigrate to Canada from Scotland in 1815 22

1817 Return of Catholics from New Ross to Eastern Canada 23

Immigrants Proceeding to Upper Canada from New York 1817-1819 24

Passengers Who Emigrated to Canada between 1817 and 1849 25

Immigration Lists 1817-1896 26

List of persons engaged to go to Red River Settlement 20 March 1819 27

Inmates from England in the New York City Almshouse 1819-1830 Who First Sailed to Canada 29

St. Lawrence Steamboat Co. Passenger Records 1819-1836 31

3

1819-1840 Alms House Admission Records 32

Scottish Settlers to Quebec 31 May 1820 34

Records of Emigrant Agent James Allison 1823-1849 35

1825 Peter Robinson Settlers 36

Emigrants from Arran Scotland to Upper Canada 1829 39

Emigrants in Ops Township, October 1829 41

Ship Euphrosyne from Heytesbury Scotland to Quebec 24 March 1831 44

Toronto Emigrant Office Assisted Immigration 1831-1892 46

Immigrants Sponsored by the Montreal Emigrant Society, 1832 47

Irish Immigrants at Grosse-Île 1832-1937 49

Petworth Immigrants 1832-1837 50

English Emigrants on board The Kingston intending to settle in Hull Township Lower Canada 1834 51

Destitute Immigrants at Prescott 1835 53

Destitute & Sick Immigrants at Prescott 1835 57

Poor Law Union Immigration from England to Canada 1836-1853 60

1840s Emigration from Wicklow Ireland to Canada 62

Canada Company Remittance Books 1843-1847 63

Emigrants from the 1845-1847 Records of James Allison .. 64

Orphan Children in charge of the Montreal Protestant Orphan Asylum 1847 66

Passenger Books of J & J Cooke 1847-1871 69

Fitzwilliam Estate Immigrants 1847-1855 70

Emigration Agent Returns of Emigrant Orphans, 1847 71

New York Almshouse Inmates in 1850-1855 who first arrived in Canada 72

Kingston Ontario Arrivals 1861-1882 73

Index to Miscellaneous Immigrants to Canada Before 1865 74

Colonial Archives Database 75

Where Are the Ships Passenger Lists for Canada Before 1865?

Before 1865 passenger lists for ships arriving at ports in Canada did not have to be archived. It is therefore a challenging time period in which to find passenger lists.

The good news is that there are alternate records such as shipping agent records, emigration agent ledger books and newspaper extracts, to name a few. These records may record your ancestor's name showing his or her arrival.

Finding these alternate records is not an easy task. Some are online but a few are only available offline in Archives or Museums. This book has gathered together all known resources for those pre-1865 passenger lists. Each item in this book provides a brief overview of what is in each record set and where it can be found. As well I have transcribed some passenger lists exclusively for this book and have not published them online.

It is important to note that outgoing passenger lists were not often kept by the originating port of departure so for the most part you must rely on inbound lists and alternate records for arrivals in Canada in this time period.

Most of the links provided in this booklet take the reader to free websites. The few that are not free but require payment of some sort are marked as such.

How Can I Find My Ancestor's Year of Immigration?

Beyond the few remaining ships passenger lists and alternate immigration records for this pre-1865 time period, there are a few ways you can narrow the timeline for your ancestor's arrival.

Some areas (townships or other smaller locales within a province) took a nominal census where the number of years a person had been in the province was noted. For example there is an 1842 census for Ontario which records the number of years all foreign-born members of the household had been in the province.

Certain census asked for an immigration date. For example the 1901 and 1911 Canadian census asked for an immigration year. Bear in mind however that immigration years are one of the most mis-remembered dates! Thus the given year is often out by several years. It is a good idea to add 5 years on either side of the recorded date when you conduct a search in other records.

Checking land records is another good way to try to narrow the timeline for an ancestor's arrival in Canada. Many settlers purchased land soon after they arrived so you will want to hunt for details of when and where he purchased land.

Sometimes you will find an early census record showing your ancestor having children born in the country of origin and in Canada. If children were born fairly close together you will have a narrow time frame for immigration.

1801 A List of Names Going Through to Upper Canada From New Brunswick

From a letter written by Thomas Barclay in New York on September 16, 1801, and received at Quebec on December 25th of the same year. The letter reads in part

Extracted from a letter from Thomas Barclay, written in New York on September 16, 1801, and received at Quebec on December 25th of the same year. Letter reads in part *"The enclosed list contains the names of four families who have removed from the Province of New Brunswick with an intention of forming a settlement in Upper Canada and who are connected with each other by several intermarriages.... I know them to be Loyal subjects of His Majesty, several of the older branches having served during the American War in the Provincial Corps....."*

John Cronk Sr.
Abigail Cronk
John Cronk Jr., 40
John Williams Sr.
John Williams Jr., 37
Glenot? Williams
William Williams, 10
Elisabeth Williams, 8
Catherine Williams, 6
James Williams, 4
Ann Williams, 1
Peleg Underwood
Susanna Underwood
John Underwood, 8
Peleg Underwood Jr., 6

James Underwood, 3
Joseph Underwood, 1
Jeremiah Traveys/Travis?
Elisabeth Traveys/Travis?
William Traveys/Travis? 10
Matthew Traveys/Travis? 8
Whitney Traveys/Travis? 6
Joshua Traveys/Travis? 4
Elisabeth Traveys/Travis? 2
Daniel Traveys/Travis? 1

Image can be viewed at
http://olivetreegenealogy.com/Ebooks/1801NB/

Passengers from Lachine to Selkirk's Baldoon Settlement Kent County, Ontario 1804

A historic plaque provides a description of the Baldoon Settlement

On September 5, 1804, fifteen families of Scottish emigrants numbering some ninety persons landed near this site. Named after an estate in Scotland, the settlement was sponsored by Lord Selkirk who later founded the Red River Colony. The low-lying and frequently flooded lands were difficult to work, malaria killed many settlers and the superintendent, Alexander McDonell, proved incapable. In July, 1812, the colony was invaded by American militia who carried off its livestock. The remaining settlers ultimately moved back to higher land and in 1818 Selkirk sold his property.

- BROWN Alexander
- BROWN Donald
- BROWN Flora
- BROWN Hector
- BROWN Marion
- BUCHANNAN Alexander
- BUCHANNAN Donald
- BUCHANNAN John
- BUCHANNAN John
- BUCHANNAN Kath.
- BUCHANNAN Kath.
- BUCHANNAN Marion
- BUCHANNAN Nelly
- BUCHANNAN Robert
- MORRISON Peggy

- MORRISON   James
- MORRISON   Flora
- MORRISON   Christian
- MORRISON   Charles
- MacCALLUM   Amelia
- MacCALLUM   Ann
- MacCALLUM   Donald
- MacCALLUM   Flora
- MacCALLUM   Hugh
- MacCALLUM   Johanna
- MacCALLUM   Mary
- MacCALLUM   Peggy
- MacDONALD   Sarah
- MacDONALD   Ruth
- MacDONALD   Peter
- MacDONALD   Peter
- MacDONALD   Peggy
- MacDONALD   Nice
- MacDONALD   Neil
- McDONALD   Mary
- MacDONALD   Mary
- MacDONALD   Mary
- MacDONALD   Mary
- MacDONALD   Mary
- MacDONALD   Kerety
- MacDONALD   Kath.
- MacDONALD   Kath.
- MacDONALD   Kath.
- MacDONALD   John
- MacDONALD   John
- MacDONALD   John
- MacDONALD   John
- MacDONALD   Jean
- MacDONALD   Hugh
- MacDONALD   Hector
- MacDONALD   Flora

- MacDONALD Flora
- MacDONALD Duncan
- MacDONALD Donald
- MacDONALD Donald
- MacDONALD Donald
- MacDONALD David
- MacDONALD Archibald
- MacDONALD Ann
- MacDONALD Angus
- MacDONALD Angus
- MacDONALD Angus
- MacDONALD Angus
- MacDONALD Angus
- MacDONALD Andrew
- MacDONALD Ance
- MacDONALD Allan
- MacDONALD Alexander
- MacDOUGALD Sarah
- MacDOUGALD Munly
- McDOUGALD Mary
- MacDOUGALD Lauchlan
- MacDOUGALD John
- McDOUGALD John
- MacDOUGALD James
- MacDOUGALD Hector
- MacDOUGALD Flora
- MacDOUGALD Archibald
- MacDOUGALD Ann
- MacDOUGALD Angus
- MacDOUGALD Allan
- MacKAY Flora
- McKENZIE Keneth
- McKENZIE John
- McKENZIE Flora
- McKENZIE Donald
- McKENZIEAnn

- McLAUGHLIN Nancy
- MacLEAN Mary
- McLEAN Mary
- MacLEAN Kersty
- MacLEAN Hector
- McLEAN Effie
- MacLEAN Ann
- MacLEAN Allan
- MacPHERSON Mary
- McPHERSON Kerety
- MacPHERSON Dugald
- McPHERSON Donald
- MacPHERSON Angus
- MacPHERSON Alexander

List of Baldoon Settlers and their children, 1809

Historical Plaque Text

On September 5, 1804, fifteen families of Scottish emigrants numbering some ninety persons landed near this site. Named after an estate in Scotland, the settlement was sponsored by Lord Selkirk who later founded the Red River Colony. The low-lying and frequently flooded lands were difficult to work, malaria killed many settlers and the superintendent, Alexander McDonell, proved incapable. In July 1812 the colony was invaded by American militia who carried off its livestock. The remaining settlers ultimately moved back to higher land and in 1818 Selkirk sold his property.

McDonald	Peter
McDonald	John
McDonald	David
McDonald	Peter
McDonald	Alexander
McDonald	John
McDonald	Angus
McDonald	Neil
McDonald	Unice
McDonald	Catherine
McDonald	Donald
McDonald	Angus
McDonald	Christy
McDonald	Mary
McDonald	Flora
McDonald	Peggy
McCallum	Donald
McCallum	Hugh

McCallum	Bell
McCallum	Peggy
McCallum	Nancy
McDougall	John
McDougall	Sarah
McDougall	John
McDougall	Hector
McDougall	Hector
McDougall	Archibald
McDougall	James
McDougall	Flora
McPherson	Angus
McPherson	Christy
McPherson	Alexander
McPherson	Donald
McPherson	Dougald
McPherson	Mary
McDonald	Angus
McDonald	Nancy
McDonald	John
McDonald	Archibald
McDonald	Donald
McDonald	Hector
McDonald	Neil
Buchanan	John
Brown	Christina
Buchanan	Alexander
Buchanan	Donald
Buchanan	John
Buchanan	Catherine
Buchanan	Nelly
Brown	Donald
McDougall	Allan
McDougall	Nancy
McDougall	John
McDougall	Mary
McDougall	Margaret

Brown	Donald
Brown	Christina
Brown	Neil
Brown	Hector
Brown	Alexander
Brown	Hugh
Brown	Colin
Morrison	Charles
Morrison	Peggy
Morrison	James
Morrison	Flora
Morrison	Christy
Morrison	Bell
McKenzie	John
McKenzie	Nancy
McKenzie	Kenneth
McKenzie	John
McDonald	Donald
McDonald	Flora
McDonald	John
McDonald	Duncan
McDonald	Hugh
McDonald	Alexander
McDonald	Angus
McDonald	Jean
McDonald	Andrew
McDonald	Catherine
McDonald	Nancy
McLean	Allan
McLean	Mary
McLean	Hector
McLean	Catherine
McLean	Mary
McLean	Henrietta
McDonell	Angus
McDougall	Mary
McDonell	John

McDonald   Allan
McKay   Bell
McDougall Angus

Microfilm Reel Number: C-14 Reference: MG 19 E1

Passengers from Lachine to Selkirk's Baldoon Settlement in Kent County, Ontario 1812

A historic plaque provides a description of the Baldoon Settlement

On September 5, 1804, fifteen families of Scottish emigrants numbering some ninety persons landed near this site. Named after an estate in Scotland, the settlement was sponsored by Lord Selkirk who later founded the Red River Colony. The low-lying and frequently flooded lands were difficult to work, malaria killed many settlers and the superintendent, Alexander McDonell, proved incapable. In July, 1812, the colony was invaded by American militia who carried off its livestock. The remaining settlers ultimately moved back to higher land and in 1818 Selkirk sold his property.

The 1812 records contain remarks about status, age and character of the Baldoon settlers made by the agent Alexander McDonell. Here is an example of what Agent McDonell wrote about one settler named John McDougall Sr:

- *John McDougall Sr. dead*
- *Allan, his son, Seaman, clever but not steady, not particularly drunken but frolicsome. Quarrelsome but not ill-disposed, married in Scotland, 4 or 5 children*
- *Angus, married Flora McCallum, well-behaved, ---*
- *John, married W. Thomson, good lad, very --*
- *Hector, 20, very good lad, good workman, not steady, wrangling*
- *Lauchlin, 16? , wild*

- *Nel, 10, spoilt by his mother*
- *James, 8, ditto*

Alphabetical List of Settlers

Brown	Alexander
Brown	Donald
Brown	Hector
Brown	John
Brown	Neil
Buchanan	Alexander
Buchanan	John
Buchanan	John
Buchanan	John
McCallum	Donald
McCallum	Flora
McCallum	Hugh
McDonald	Alexander
McDonald	Allan
McDonald	Angus
McDonald	Angus
McDonald	Angus
McDonald	Angus
McDonald	Angus
McDonald	Angus
McDonald	Archibald
Mcdonald	David
McDonald	Donald
McDonald	Donald
McDonald	Donald
McDonald	Hector
McDonald	John
McDonald	John
Mcdonald	John
McDonald	John
McDonald	Neil

McDonald	Neil
McDonald	Peter
McDonald	Peter
McDougal	Allan
McDougal	Angus
McDougal	Hector
McDougal	James
McDougal	John
McDougal	John Senior
McDougal	Lauchlin
McDougal	Neil
McKenzie	Donald
McKenzie	John
McKenzie	Kenneth
McLean	Allan
McLean	Hector
McPherson	Alexander
McPherson	Angus
McPherson	Donald
McPherson	Dugald
Morrison	Charles
Morrison	James

Reference: Selkirk collection C-19. Images with full details on each individual may be consulted at Canadian's Heritage Collection. There is no index available but I have found the start of the settler details. It is found at:
http://heritage.canadiana.ca/view/oocihm.lac_reel_c19/416?r=0&s=1

New Brunswick Passenger Lists 1815-1838

These records consist of Saint John New Brunswick Customs House Passenger Lists from 1815, 1832, 1833-1834 & 1837-1838

These lists appear to be the only surviving passenger records for the port of Saint John for this period, and contain the names of more than 10,500 passengers and crew (some men worked their passage).

Most of the Customs House records were lost in 1877 in the Great Fire of Saint John. Famine lists from 1845-1850 appear also to have been lost.

Consult
http://www.theshipslist.com/ships/passengerlists/saintjohnindex.shtml

Settlers intending to emigrate to Canada from Scotland in 1815

This is a General List of Settlers enrolled for Canada under the Government Regulations at Edinburgh 1815

The Colonial Office "Master" List is comprised of 757 names (699 of whom sailed) with full details of those intending to emigrate to Canada, and the corresponding Canadian arrival lists showing head of household, and numbers and age-range of accompanying family.

The lists are available online for the Atlas (sailed from Greenock July 11th 1815, and arriving at Quebec September 4th 1815), Dorothy (sailed from Greenock July 12th 1815, arriving at Quebec September 4th 1815) & Baltic Merchant (ailed from Greenock July 14th 1815, arriving at Quebec September 4th 1815). The Eliza (sailed from Greenock August 3rd 1815, arrival date at Quebec not known) arrival list did not survive but a reconstructed list is available.

Consult http://www.theshipslist.com/ships/passengerlists/edinburgh index.shtml

1817 Return of Catholics from New Ross to Eastern Canada

A Return of Catholic (Wexford Carlow) families who sailed from New Ross to Upper Eastern Canada in Nov 1817. The return lists 1,475 individuals representing 281 Roman Catholic Families who left New Ross 29 November 1817

Included are the names of the head of the family, occupation, total number in the family and religion.

Consult
http://www.ancestorsatrest.com/ireland_genealogy_data/ireland_to_canada_1817.shtml

Immigrants Proceeding to Upper Canada from New York 1817-1819

This is a set of passes for recent immigrants from the United Kingdom (England, Scotland, Wales and Ireland) who arrived in New York but are continuing on to Upper Canada (present day Ontario).

A few passes include the name of the ship the immigrant sailed on. The value of this obscure set of records lies with its recording of the exact date the immigrant applied for his or her pass. This provides researchers with a very good idea of immigration from the U.K.

It may not be possible to find the actual ship that an immigrant sailed on as ships passenger lists into U.S.A. (except for Pennsylvania) did not have to be kept prior to 1820. Presumably most of these immigrants arrived via New York.

There are 199 passes on the digitized microfilm, and the extracted list of names with details is available as a free database at

http://www.olivetreegenealogy.com/ships/canada/Immigrants%20New%20York%20to%20Canada1817.shtml

Each indexed name on the site above has the information needed for a researcher to easily view the actual image of the immigrant's pass.

Passengers Who Emigrated to Canada between 1817 and 1849

This is an index taken from passenger lists of more than 3,000 names found in the British Colonial Office records. A typical record consists of the name of an individual, date of arrival in Canada, and details to obtain his or her full record on microfilm.

There is no online index available but you may request a lookup for a small fee for the record at

http://www.olivetreegenealogy.com/ships/canada/lookups-immigration.shtml

Immigration Lists 1817-1896

This collection is made up largely of correspondence and dispatches regarding emigration from the British Isles to Canada. While some of the correspondence relates to immigration in general, this database also includes letters from many individuals requesting information and assistance to immigrate to Canada.

You may find military service noted, families mentioned, and the socio-economic circumstances of the author. Volume 2 from the entry books contains a list of 757 Scottish settlers who immigrated to Canada.

(Pay to view) To search the database, see

http://search.ancestry.ca/search/db.aspx?dbid=3709

List of persons engaged to go to Red River Settlement 20 March 1819

In 1812 the Hudson's Bay Company gave Lord Selkirk a land grant of 116,000 acres at the junction of the Red and Assiniboine Rivers in the Red River Valley. The plan was for Selkirk to bring in Scottish settlers. Many farmers came from the county of Sutherland and the Orkney Islands in Scotland joined by Scottish farmers from the Western Highlands and Islands who were being pushed off their lands.

Selkirk did not have trouble finding Irish and Scottish settlers to come and live in the Red River Settlement. The first settlers, who arrived in 1812, faced much hardship. Many decided to leave for Upper Canada, where they could find better land a more agreeable climate.

The microfilmed lists contain details of each settler including their parish or town of origin. I have abstracted the names below and arranged them in alphabetical order below.

BELL Helen
BROCKIE Gideon, ploughman
BROWN Martha
BURNET John, ploughman
CAMPBELL Robert, ploughman
GEDDES Robert, ploughman
HAIG Jane
KNOX   Michael, ploughman
LANDRETH George, ploughman
MERCER Robert, ploughman
MITCHELL John, gardener

OVENS Edward, ploughman
PARK   Joseph, Carpenter
SHAW   Betsy
TELFER John, ploughman
TALLY David,Smith

The microfilm C-6 has been digitized and is online but there is no index available. I searched to find the list for these Red River Settlers in 1819. You can view it at http://heritage.canadiana.ca/view/oocihm.lac_reel_c6/397?r=0&s=1

Inmates from England in the New York City Almshouse 1819-1830 Who First Sailed to Canada

In the 1800s many people left England and sailed to America or Canada. Some ended up impoverished in a City Almshouse or Poorhouse. I have extracted the names of 254 English immigrants who ended up in the New York City Almshouse between 1818 and 1830. This includes the name of the ship they sailed on (when known)

In the early 1800's port cities in the USA bore the burden of immigration. By the time they arrived, so many immigrants were tired, hungry and poor they ended up in the City Almshouse. This meant the citizens had to take care of them.

Dating back to the colonial era, New York City assumed responsibility for its citizens who were destitute, sick, homeless, or otherwise unable to care for themselves. The city maintained an almshouse, various hospitals, and a workhouse on Blackwell's Island (now called Roosevelt Island) for the poor.

There are 2 pages for each name in the original ledger. I have only copied part of the left hand page. There is more information on the original microfilm, including Captain's Name, Owner's Name, Date of Bond, Sureties, Date Discharged, Death Date, Remarks, Bonded, Commuted & Total.

See http://www.allenglishrecords.com/almshouse-a-f.shtml

St. Lawrence Steamboat Co. Passenger Records 1819-1836

One method of proceeding inward (west) and down (south) into the United States, after arriving by Sailing Ship at the port of Quebec, was to take passage in one of the St. Lawrence Steamboat Co. Steamers to Montreal.

Some records of passengers exist for the years 1819 to 1836, on the Steamers Malsham, New Swiftsure, Lady Sherbrooke, Car of Commerce, Caledonia, Quebec, Telegraph, Chambly, Waterloo, John Molson, St. Lawrence, John Bull, Canada, Voyageur and Canadian Eagle.

Each of these ships made several voyages over the years. Typically you'll find the name of the passenger, abbreviations for ports of embarkation and destination, fare, amount paid, and remarks. You can also see whether they were traveling in steerage or in a cabin, and the dates of travel.

For lists of passengers consult
http://www.theshipslist.com/ships/passengerlists/1819_20index.shtml

(Pay to view) For lists of passengers including images of original manifests see
http://search.ancestry.ca/search/db.aspx?dbid=3612

1819-1840 Alms House Admission Records

The Alms House Admission Foreigners & Nativity Records with Ships Names 1819 - 1840 (New York City, New York) Includes individuals who had sailed into Canada first before arriving in New York

In the early 1800's port cities in the USA bore the burden of immigration. By the time they arrived, so many immigrants were tired, hungry and poor they ended up in the City Almshouse. This meant the citizens had to take care of them. At first the citizens of the city asked the Mayors for funds to support the poor. Eventually they asked the states, and by mid-century some states (PA, NY, MA) set up State agencies to deal with the issue. Eventually, beginning in the 1880's, the Federal Government nationalized the programs.

Dating back to the colonial era, New York City assumed responsibility for its citizens who were destitute, sick, homeless, or otherwise unable to care for themselves. The city maintained an almshouse, various hospitals, and a workhouse on Blackwell's Island (now called Roosevelt Island) for the poor.

There are 2 pages for each name in this ledger. Only information from the left hand page of the ledger is online. There is more information on the original microfilm, including Captain's Name, Owner's Name, Date of Bond, Sureties, Date Discharged, Death Date, Remarks, Bonded, Commuted & Total.

Ship arrivals with partial passenger names before October 1819 include Ann, Caroline, Cleatham, Cossack, Dublin Packet, Ellerd, Emulation, Felix or Phoenix, Iris, John Dickinson, Little Bill, Margaret, Nancy, Ontario, Phoenix, Prudence, Rosella, The Otis, Visitor

Consult
http://www.olivetreegenealogy.com/ships/ny_alms1819.shtml

Scottish Settlers to Quebec 31 May 1820

Names and Numbers of Souls in the Abercrombie Friendly Emigration Society who agree to pay their passage to Quebec, counting all ages. Glasgow 31 May 1820.

The image at http://www.olivetreegenealogy.com/Ebooks/Scots1820/Abercrombie31May-702.jpg provides the following details:

Name of head of family plus whether or not a wife is with them, number of children under 2 years of age, children ages 2 to 14, children older than 14 and total number in family

Walter Beatie
Daniel Dempster
James Dobie
William Gordon
John Lotton
James McDonald
William McDonald
James McDougald
Samuel Wilson

Total number of men, women and children is 40.

Records of Emigrant Agent James Allison 1823-1849

This database consists of the records of James Allison, Emigrant Agent at Montreal, 1823-1845 Vol. 21 and 1846-1849 Vol. 22

About 75 pages of this collection consist of lists with names of emigrants. These lists have been indexed and are searchable by name. In addition to their name other information that may be listed about the emigrants includes:

- Date of ticket

- Number of adults, children, and infants in party

- Destination

(Pay to view) To search these records see

http://search.ancestry.ca/search/db.aspx?dbid=1553

1825 Peter Robinson Settlers

Ships passenger lists for Peter Robinson Settlers sailing 1825 Ireland to Canada This online set of records includes passenger lists and surgeon's logs of the sick and dying, plus Survey Responses from 180 settlers 1823-1825

In 1822, the British Government established a trial emigration scheme for Irish paupers to Upper Canada. There were two waves of emigration, one in 1823 the second in 1825.

On July 1, 1823, Peter Robinson arranged for 568 paupers from Ireland (mainly Cork) to sail on two ships, the Hebe and the Stakesby, to Quebec City. Each ship carried an experienced medical officer. Following an eight-week sea voyage, the passengers boarded steamships, then barges, and wagons for the rest of the journey to Upper Canada (present day Ontario). They settled in the Townships of Ramsay, Pakenham, Bathurst, Lanark, Beckwith, Goulbourn, Darling and Huntley in the Ottawa Valley area.

In spring of 1825, Robinson recorded 2024 passengers on board nine ships - Fortitude, Resolution, Albion, Brunswick, Star, Amity, Regulus, Elizabeth, and John Barry. The ships left Cobh, Cork Harbor Ireland in May and June, 1825. By the fall of 1825, each family was relocated to a log shanty on property in – Asphodel, Douro, Dummer, Emily, Ennismore (Gore of Emily), Smith, and Otonabee Townships in Peterborough.

The following passenger lists are online

- Surgeon's Journal of the Transport Ship John Barry between 22 April to 25 July 1825 during which time the said ship has been employed in conveying the Irish Emigrant Settlers from Cork to Quebec.

- Surgeon's Journal of the Transport Ship Amity between 5 April to 9 July 1825 during which time the said ship has been employed in conveying the Irish Emigrant Settlers from Cork to Quebec
- Surgeon's Journal of the Transport Ship Elizabeth between 4 May 1825 & 21st July 1825 during which time the said ship has been employed in conveying the Irish Emigrant Settlers from Cork to Quebec.
- Medical and surgical journal of the Star transport ship for 6 April to 13 July 1825 by Ninian McMorris, Surgeon and Superintendent, during which time the said ship was employed in conveying emigrants to Quebec.
- Journal of the Medical and surgical journal of the Regulus transport ship for 7 April to 13 July 1825 by Matthew Burnside, Surgeon and Superintendent conveying the Irish Emigrant Settlers from Cork to Quebec
- Medical and surgical journal of the Fortitude Emigrant Ship for 28 April to 1 July 1825 by Francis Connin, Surgeon and Superintendent conveying the Irish Emigrant Settlers from Cork to Quebec.
- Medical journal of the Brunswick, emigrant ship, for 5 April to 27 June 1825 by John Tarn surgeon and superintendent, during which time the said ship was employed in conveying emigrants from Cork to Quebec
- Medical and surgical journal of the Albion Convict Ship, for 4 April to 4 July 1825 by John Thomson Surgeon and Superintendent, during which time the said vessel was employed in conveying emigrants from Cork to Quebec
- Passenger List of Fortitude May 1825 Cork Ireland with final destination Peterborough Ontario
- Passenger List of Resolution May 1825 Cork Ireland with final destination Peterborough Ontario

- Passenger List of Star May 1825 Cork Ireland with final destination Peterborough Ontario
- Passenger List of Elizabeth May 1825 Cork Ireland with final destination Peterborough Ontario
- Passenger List of Albion May 1825 Cork Ireland with final destination Peterborough Ontario
- Passenger List of Brunswick May 1825 Cork Ireland with final destination Peterborough Ontario
- Passenger List of Amity May 1825 Cork Ireland with final destination Peterborough Ontario
- Passenger List of Regulus May 1825 Cork Ireland with final destination Peterborough Ontario

Consult
http://www.olivetreegenealogy.com/ships/canada/PeterRobinson.shtml

Emigrants from Arran Scotland to Upper Canada 1829

28 Feb. 1829. List of names of those intending to go this Spring, from Arran to Upper Canada

Note that Arran is the Isle of Arran in the Firth of Clyde, Scotland.

Details include name of head of family, occupation, residence, age plus age of wife and numbers and ages of sons and daughters. Example: Archibald McKillop, farmer and fish curer, Lochranza, age 47, wife 39, 2 sons and 5 daughters age from 18 years to 10 months

Archibald McKillop, 47
Archibald McKillop, 52
Charles Murdoch, 41
Archibald Melso, 47
Donald McKillop, 54
Niel McKillop, 61
Alexander Kelso, 39
John McKenzie, 39
William McKenzie, 43
Francis Logan, 30
Robert Kelso, 47
Margaret Kelso, 54, widow, and son Malcolm 18, son James 15
Angus Brodie, 34
William Kelso, 42
Dugald McKenzie, 31
Niel McMillan, 42
Peter Sillars, 40

Catherine Kelso, 36 widow
James Fullarton, 36
Peter McKillop, 32
Bell Crawford, 48, widow
Archibald McKenzie, 36
Duncan Stewart, 56
Donald McIntyre, 50
Mrs. Murhie
Peter McKenzie

Images at
http://www.olivetreegenealogy.com/Ebooks/Scots1829/

Emigrants in Ops Township, October 1829

List of emigrants located in the Township of Ops by Mr. A. McDonell up to the 15th of October 1829. This list is found in Upper Canada Sundries and contains information as to land location as well as the information I extracted below.

Note that there is no index for the Upper Canada Land Sundries but I found the start of the list at http://heritage.canadiana.ca/view/oocihm.lac_reel_c6868/1259?r=0&s=1

Image 1259 p.53981 is the first page of the list

- Terence Brady, Mary Brady, wife, Thomas Brady 3, Michael Brady 1 3/4
- ? Black, single man
- James Brennan, single man
- Patrick Brennan, a wife and 4 children
- Oliver Burke, single man
- Barnet Clarke, single man
- James Clarke, single man
- Patrick Dunn, John Dunn, brother, Mary Dunn, sister, Mary Dunn, mother, Michael Dunn, brother

- John Fallen, Mary Fallen, wife, Margaret Fallen 5, Bertrand Fallen   2
- Duncan Fisher, Margaret Fisher wife, Anne Fisher sister, Catharine Fisher mother, Peter Fisher 4 ½, Donald Fisher 2 ½, John Fisher   1
- Patrick Hannoran, Bridget Hannoran, Catharine Hannoran 14, John Hannoran 2

- Patrick Hoey, Nicholas Hoey, brother,Thomas Hoey , brother
- Brien Hoey, Mary Hoey, wife,Catharine Hoey 14, Patrick Hoey 1
- Cornelius Hogan, family at the Rideau Canal

- Martin Hogan, family at the Rideau Canal

- Daniel Hyde, family in United States, 5 in number
- Hyde's son in law, family in United States, 2 in number
- William Johnston, Mary Johnston, wife
- William Jones, single man
- Mr. Jones, single man
- William Lee, Elizabeth Lee, wife, Mary Lee 15, Hannah Lee 8, Sam'l Lee 8, John Lee 6
- Robert Miller, family in Ireland
- Thomas Miller, family in Ireland
- Francis McCabe family in Ireland, will join him next Spring
- Alexander McCarthy, Elizabeth McCarthy wife, John McCarthy 19, Margaret McCarthy 15
- Robert Martin, family in Ireland expected next spring

- Peter Morrison, John Morrison 10, Hugh Morrison 3 ½, James Morrison 1, Margaret Morrison wife
- John Murray, Mary Murray, mother, James Murray, brother, Matthew Murray, brother, Patrick Murray, brother, Peter Murray, brother, Philip Murray, brother, Catharine Murray, sister, Ann Murray, sister, Margaret Murray, sister
- James Narney, Catharine Narney wife, Jane Narney 19, Anne Narney 18, Charles Narney 14, Thomas Narney 6, Mary Narney 3
- Samuel Parkins, Mary Parkins, wife, Mary Parkins 19, Anthony Parkins 11, Anne Parkins 9, Martha Parkins 7, Charles Parkins 3, Hannah Parkins 1

- James Payne, Catharine Payne, wife, James Payne 19, William Payne 18, John Payne 13, Margaret Payne 9, Thomas Payne 7, Catharine Payne 3, Johanna Payne 1 ½
- John Quigley, family at the Rideau Canal

- Brien Smith, land with John Smith
- John Smith, land with Brien Smith
- Michael Smith, a wife and child
- Denis Toohey, Catharine Toohey, wife, Patrick Toohey 21, John Toohey 19, Mary Toohey 14, Daniel Toohey 11, Denis Toohey 8, James Toohey 5, Julia Toohey 3

Ship Euphrosyne from Heytesbury Scotland to Quebec 24 March 1831

A list of Emigrants from Heytesbury and its hamlets to embark for Quebec on their way to Upper Canada on 24th March 1831 on the Ship Euphrosyne. To embark at Bridgewater

Full details include name of head of family, Parish or Hamlet, Number of men + age, Number of women + age, Number of boys + age, Number of girls + age, Total adults, Total ages 7-14, Total ages under 7, Grand Total, Trade & Remark

William Bevan, Tytherington, 30
William Coleman, Heytesbury, 31
Charles Dyer, Heytesbury, 19
William Farley, Heytesbury, 17
Joseph Farley, Heytesbury, 23
David Foyle, Tytherington, 17
Henry Holland, Heytesbury, 20
Henry Hinton, Heytesbury, 21
Leonard Hinton, Heytesbury, 25
James Holland, Heytesbury, 25
John Hooker, Heytesbury, 17
William Huselle, Heytesbury, 23
William King, Tytherington, 50
James Kite, Tytherington, 19
George Miller, Tytherington, 19
Jeffrey Nokis, Heytesbury, 32
Felix Parker, Tytherington, 19
Joel Paune, Tytherington, 25
James Payne, Knoske, 24

Thomas Smith, Heytesbury, 18
John Young, Heytesbury, 23

Toronto Emigrant Office Assisted Immigration 1831-1892

The first emigrant office in Upper Canada was opened in 1833 in Toronto, headed by **AB Hawke.** The letterbooks of Chief Emigrant Agent Anthony B. Hawke are available at the Archives of Ontario from 1831 to 1892.

This database is an index to the four volumes of assisted immigration registers created by the **Toronto Emigrant Office** between **1865 and 1883**. The registers are a chronological listing of those new immigrants who were assisted by the government to travel to many different destinations across southern Ontario. Over 29,000 entries have been transcribed from the registers.

To search the database consult
http://www.archives.gov.on.ca/en/db/hawke.aspx

The 1831-1865 records are not online but can be consulted at the Archives of Ontario, 134 Ian Macdonald Boulevard, Toronto, Ontario, Canada

Immigrants Sponsored by the Montreal Emigrant Society, 1832

RETURN OF THE POOR AND DESTITUTE EMIGRANTS FORWARDED AND RELIEVED BY THE MONTREAL EMIGRANT SOCIETY FROM 23RD MAY 1832 TO 1ST NOVEMBER 1832.

Library and Archives Canada holds the register of names of immigrants for the year 1832 from the Montreal Emigrant Society (RG 7 G18) (available on microfilm reel H-962). This is the only register from the Montreal Emigrant Society held by Library and Archives Canada. This register has been scanned and digitized images are accessible online.

The register for 1832 contains the following information:

- Ticket Number
- Names
- Age - Above 60
- Age - Above 40
- Age - Above 20
- Children - Over 14 years
- Children - Under 14 years
- Children - Under 7 years
- Children - Infants
- Where From
- Where Sent
- Occupation or Trade
- Rations - Pork
- Rations - Biscuit
- Rations - Oatmeal
- Remarks

The searchable database provides access to 1,947 references to the Montreal Emigrant Society Passage Book for 1832 held at Library and Archives Canada. Names of passengers are connected to images of the actual register. You can print the images or save the images on your own computer.

http://www.bac-lac.gc.ca/eng/discover/immigration/immigration-records/immigrants-montreal-emigrant-society/Pages/introduction.aspx

Irish Immigrants at Grosse-Île 1832-1937

This set of records consists of a list of immigrants whose names appear in surviving records of the Grosse-Île Quarantine Station between 1832 and 1937.

Around 1830, an average of 30,000 immigrants arrived annually in the City of Québec, the main port of entry to Canada. Approximately two-thirds of these newcomers were from Ireland. This immigration on the St. Lawrence River took place at a time when major cholera and smallpox epidemics were sweeping through Europe. In order to help control the spread of the diseases, the quarantine station at Grosse Île, located in the St. Lawrence River downstream from the City of Québec, was established in 1832 and operated until its closure in 1937.

The database contains 33,036 references to immigrants who stayed, were born, married or buried at the Grosse Île Quarantine Station between 1832 and 1937. The database also includes references to immigrants who were born or died at sea during those years. It also includes references to immigration workers and their families who were living on the island.

http://www.bac-lac.gc.ca/eng/discover/immigration/immigration-records/immigrants-grosse-ile-1832-1937/Pages/immigrants-grosse-ile.aspx

Petworth Immigrants 1832-1837

In the 1830s, English parishes and landlords tried to solve problems of rural poverty by assisting people to emigrate to Upper Canada.

The Petworth Emigration Committee chartered ships and sent emigrants from England to Canada in each of the six years between 1832 and 1837. In addition to people from its own Petworth area of Sussex, the committee helped send emigrants from almost 100 parishes in Sussex and neighbouring counties.

Between 1830 and 1837, more than 19,000 immigrants arriving at the port of Quebec had had financial help from parishes and landlords.

The ships which brought the settlers over were:

- 1832- Eveline, Lord Melville, England, Brunswick
- 1833 - England
- 1834 - British Tar
- 1835 - Burrell
- 1836 - Heber
- 1837 - Diana

You may view these records at http://www.theshipslist.com/ships/passengerlists/petworth.shtml and at http://www.petworthemigrations.com/

English Emigrants on board The Kingston intending to settle in Hull Township Lower Canada 1834

This is a list of emigrants on board the Kingston from Liverpool, who accompanied William Farmer of Brockton Court, Shropshire, to settle in Hull Township, Lower Canada.

William Farmer (1794-1880) was a Shropshire farmer who emigrated to Canada in 1834 in the Kingston of Liverpool, a vessel which he chartered to transport his party of 55 persons, which included his wife, children, servants and their families, as well as 56 head of farming stock, and all their farming equipment, furniture and other possessions. From the Wright family, William Farmer leased the Gatineau Falls farm in Hull Township, Lower Canada, about six miles from Bytown, and tried to establish a sawmilling business on the Gatineau River. The enterprise failed, however, and had to be turned over to Alonzo Wright in 1846. In 1855, Farmer and his family moved to Canada West and eventually settled at Ancaster, near Hamilton, in 1860.

Transcribed list of the names of immigrants in alphabetical order

ADDERLEY William
BARNFIELD Thomas
BONELL Amos
BONELL Catherine
BONELL Fanny
BONELL George
BONELL Thomas

BONELL	William
CHILD	Annie
CHILD	Fanny
CHILD	Mary
CHILD	Peter
CHILD	Thomas
DUKES	William
FARMER	Eleanor
FARMER	Elizabeth
FARMER	Harriet
FARMER	Jane
FARMER	Joseph
FARMER	Thomas
FARMER	William
FARMER	William
FURNIVALL	William
GREEN	James
LANGFORD	Annie
LANGFORD	Bessie
LANGFORD	Mary
LANGFORD	Richard
LANGFORD	Samuel
LANGFORD	William
PARTON	Bessie
PARTON	James
PARTON	Richard
PARTON	Thomas
RUDKINS	Jemima
SMITH	Ellen
VICKERS	Arthur
WILLIAMS	Mr. and Mrs.
WILLIAMS	James
WILLIAMS	Joseph
WILLIAMS	George

Library & Archives Canada Reference: MG 24 I 120 William Farmer and family fond

Destitute Immigrants at Prescott 1835

Return of Passages Furnished at Public Expense to Destitute Immigrants at Prescott, from the opening of navigation to 31 August 1835. Source: Upper Canada Sundries, Microfilm C-6887 page 85857

This list of Destitute Immigrants seeking passage further west in what is now Ontario has several columns: Name of immigrant; Number of Deaths and non-deaths for males and females; where they were from, where they were heading, the number of tickets issued for passage, the rate for each ticket and the total amount for passage. There is also a column for additional remarks. I have only transcribed some of the columns.

Here is my transcribed list of 33 individuals, in alphabetical order. They were not in alphabetical order on the original list. Most of them were Irish seeking to settle in Upper Canada and needing financial assistance to go further.

- ARMSTRONG John   Ireland to Port Hope   has been hurt at the Long Sault Canal and has relatives in the township of Cavan

- BARRETT Ellen   Ireland to Niagara   to join her husband who has been out 2 years

- BRIDGES George   England to Hamilton   a discharged soldier with very sore eyes, to go to his father

- CARROLL Margaret   Ireland to Niagara was wrecked in the Wm Ewen on Seateree Island

- COCKANS Edward   Ireland to Niagara was wrecked in the Wm Ewen on Seateree Island

53

- CLUNE   Mary   Ireland to Kingston was wrecked in the Wm Ewen on Seateree Island

- CULHEEN Mary   Ireland to Bellville   had a daughter who died in hospital here, and was herself sick, to join -- family

- CULKEEN   Michael   Ireland to Port Hope   A very old man, having a son in Mariposa

- DENNISON   Ann   Ireland to Toronto   to join her husband

- GALLAGHER, Margaret   Ireland to Toronto   a very old woman, say 70 years of age, to join her son

- GRAMES   Nancy   Ireland to Kingston   to join her husband

- HACKET   William   Ireland to Niagara   was wrecked in the Wm Ewen on Seateree Island

- HENRY   Sarah   Ireland to Toronto   to go to see a son residing on some part of Yonge Street

- KELLY   John   Ireland to Toronto   a young man, with 4 little boys his brothers

- LANGDON   William   England to Toronto   one of his legs very bad, has relatives in Toronto

- MONTGOMERY   John   Ireland to Kingston was wrecked in the Wm Ewen on Seateree Island

- MURRAY   Patrick   Ireland to Hamilton   has been hurt in the Canal at the Long Sault

- MURRAY   Elizabeth   Ireland to Toronto   to go to a brother living in Oakville

- McDERMOTT   Nelly   Ireland to Hamilton   widow joining a brother   1 1/2

- McGIRWIN   Nancy   Ireland to Toronto   to join her husband

- McKENNS/McFAY   Margaret   Ireland to Port Hope was wrecked in the Wm Ewen on Seateree Island

- McKENNS/McKENZIE   Niel   Ireland to Toronto   an elderly man

- McMAHON   Bernard   Ireland to Hamilton   A discharged soldier

- NIXON   John Scott   Ireland to Toronto was wrecked in the Wm Ewen on Seateree Island

- PALLS   Martha   Ireland to Toronto   a very old woman with two g--- children, to join a brother at Streetsville

- PEW   Margaret   Ireland to Toronto   has been sick in hospital here

- READ   James   Scotland to Niagara   has had very bad feet

- RODGERS   John   Ireland to Niagara   a boy, to go to his father-in-law [no doubt means step-father] and mother

- RODGERS   Joseph   Ireland to Toronto   wife lately dead, has a sister in Toronto to whom he is carrying his infant

- SCOTT   David   Ireland to Toronto   was wrecked in the Wm Ewen on Seateree Island

- SLAVER   Sally   Ireland to Niagara   was wrecked in the Wm Ewen on Seateree Island

- STRACHAN   John   Ireland to Toronto   a discharged soldier from the 9th Regiment of Foot

- WALKER   Ruth   Ireland to Toronto   a girl and a boy

See

http://www.olivetreegenealogy.com/Ebooks/Prescott1835/

Destitute & Sick Immigrants at Prescott 1835

Return of Destitute Sick Emigrants Under Medical Treatment at Prescott, from 1-31 August 1835

- ARMSTRONG   John, 33, from Ireland, diseased knee

- COLHEEN   Mary, 50, from Ireland, Rheumatism
- COLHEEN, Nancy, 20 from Ireland, Typhus Fever, died August 3, 1835
- COREY   Mary, 14, from Ireland, fever
- DENNIS   Mary, 15, from Ireland, Diarhea
- DENNIS   Patrick, 12, from Ireland, Diseased knee
- EDWARDS   Charles, 30, from England, dysentry
- HAVERIN   Bridget, 30, from Ireland, fever
- HODGES no first name , 40, from Ireland, pleurisy
- LANGDON   Mary, 4, from England, diarrhea
- LANGDON   William, 30, from England, Rheumatism
- LENE/LEWS   Mary, 8, from Ireland, convulsions
- MANSFIELD   Robert, 35, from Ireland, Typhus fever, remains under treatment
- MEA   Mary, 22, from Ireland, Inflammatory Rheumatism, remains under treatment

- MURRAY   Samuel, 46, from Ireland, Paralysis, remains under treatment

- McGIRWIN   Nancy, 24, from Ireland, fever

- McKAY/McKENNA   Margaret, 28, from Ireland, pleurisy, remains under treatment

- McMAHON   Edward, 13, from Ireland, fever

- McMICKING   Mary, 10, from Ireland, fever

- OSBORNE   Catherine, 18, from Ireland, opthalmia, remains under treatment

- PALLISER   Ann, 3, from England, diarrhea

- PALLISER   George, 6, from England, diarrhea

- PALLISSER   Mary, 8, from England, diarrhea

- PATTERSON   William, 55, from Ireland, luxation/suxation, remains under treatment

- PRINGLE   Jane, 28, from Ireland, pleurisy, remains under treatment

- PRINGLE   Margaret, 23, from Ireland, rheumatism, remains under treatment

- PRINGLE   Mary, 50, from Ireland, contusion, remains under treatment

- PUGH   Margaret, 23, from Ireland, fever

- READ   James, 42, from Scotland, Contusion

- RICHARDSON   Rebecca, 40, from Ireland, fever

- RODGERS   John, 2, from Ireland, diarrhea

- SCOTT   Jane, 32, from Ireland, diarrhea

- SCOTT, Mary, 4, from Ireland, diarrhea
- SMART/SANART   Mary, 5, from Ireland, diarrhea
- SMITH   Francis, 5, from England, diarrhea
- TORNBLETY   Mary, 3, from Ireland, diarrhea

Upper Canada Sundries
Microfilm Reel Number C-6887
Page 85853

See
http://www.olivetreegenealogy.com/Ebooks/Prescott1835/

Poor Law Union Immigration from England to Canada 1836-1853

This set of records includes the names of impoverished emigrants sent from England to Canada on board 23 ships. It also provides the names of emigrants each year from 1836 - 1871 (no ship names).

Poor law unions were collections or groups of parishes brought together to administer poor relief. The Victorian poor law was predicated on the 'workhouse test'. This is where poor relief would be offered via the 'deterrent workhouse', designed to be an institution of last resort.

In 1833 the Colonial Land and Emigration Commissioners (CLEC) were set up to manage the program of emigration to Britain's colonies (Canada, Australia, New Zealand etc.). Under the new regime, some emigrants could qualify for a free passage if they were under forty, capable of labor, of good character, having been vaccinated against smallpox, and from occupations such as agricultural laborers, shepherds, or female domestic and farm servants. Young married couples, preferably without children were viewed as the ideal candidates. Assisted passages were also available with less stringent restrictions to healthy able-bodied laborers whose moral character could be vouched for.

The records of the Poor Law Commission and the Poor Law Board are in The National Archives. They are not particularly easy to use, as the lists are very uninformative, so any search is likely to be lengthy, but it can be very rewarding. Olive Tree Genealogy has extracted the names of individuals who qualified for passage to Canada from England between the years 1836 to 1853 and in 1871. There is a gap from 1854-1870 inclusive.

The names of 23 ships are given with the names of Poor Law Union passengers. No full passenger lists for these ships are known to exist. Look for your ancestors in this online set of records at

http://www.olivetreegenealogy.com/ships/canada/PLU-ShipsIndex.shtml

1840s Emigration from Wicklow Ireland to Canada

A Story of Emigration from Southwest Wicklow (Ireland) to Ontario Canada in the 1840s with reconstructed names of immigrants can be seen at

http://www.bytown.net/wicklowemigrants.htm

Canada Company Remittance Books 1843-1847

There is a great deal of genealogical information in the Canada Company Remittance Books. The Canada Company sent money to friends and family members of settlers in Canada. The books record the receipt of the sent money in England, the recipient, the sender, and the destination. Often the occupation of the recipient is noted, as is the exact location and relationship of the sender.

This invaluable set of records in book form extracts the names of people receiving money, people sending money, where the money was sent (in care of), location of both sender and recipient, and notations of genealogical value such as *"if recipient deceased, money to go to her daughter Mary"*.

There is no online index available but you may request a lookup for a small fee for the record at

http://www.olivetreegenealogy.com/ships/canada/lookups-immigration.shtml

Emigrants from the 1845-1847 Records of James Allison

This online free database is an index of names of emigrants from the 1845-1847 records of James Allison, Emigrant Agent at Montreal

From 1823 to 1849, James Allison was a government emigrant agent at Montreal, Quebec Canada. He was responsible for the provisioning and transportation of destitute immigrants from Montreal to locations mostly in Upper Canada. There were several Emigration Agents in Upper and Lower Canada, each was responsible for assisting poor immigrants in finding employment, shelter, provisions and transportation to their final destination.

The original book *Names of Emigrants from the 1845-1847 Records of James Allison, Emigrant Agent at Montreal* is divided into two parts

Part 1: The transcript (The transcript includes the records of James Allison and an appendix from the British parliamentary papers of persons who died at Grosse Île in 1846.)

Part 2: The indexes - an Index of emigrants personal names and an Index of place names)

View the free list of names at
http://www.rootsweb.ancestry.com/~ote/ships/emigrants-montreal1845-1847a.htm

Note that the index above is not the complete record. You may also request a lookup for a small fee for the complete record at
http://www.olivetreegenealogy.com/ships/canada/lookups-immigration.shtml

Orphan Children in charge of the Montreal Protestant Orphan Asylum 1847

I have transcribed and arranged the list in alphabetical order. The register included columns for name, age, boy/girl, date of immigration, health, date of death, ship, remarks. I have transcribed name, age, date of death, ship and remarks below

Allen, Fanny, 15, Marche Butte
Batty/Barry, Catherine, 13, Lady F. Hastings,
Boyd, Thomas, 4, unknown ship, died
Campbell, Ann, 18, Christiana, ret'd to sheds with typhus
Campbell, Robert, 11, Christiana
Campbell, William, 9, Christiana
Corbon, Ann, 15, Elizabeth
Corbon, Esther, 18, Elizabeth
Corbon, Mary, 21, Elizabeth
Corson, Margaret, 25, Independent, dead
Corson, Mary Ann, 20, Independent
Corson, Nancy, 22, Independent
Davis, Grace, 10, Prince Royal
Davis, Jane, 11, Prince Royal
Davis, John, 8, Prince Royal
Diamond, Mary Ann, 12, March Abercorn
Ford, Ellen, 5, Bea
Gibson, Margaret, 5, unknown ship, died Aug.
Harrison, Mary Jane, 14, Free Trader
Johnson, Andrew, 9, July, Christiana, died
Johnson, David, 15, July, Christiana
Johnson, Elizabeth, 13, July, Christiana
Kendall, Ann, 4, unknown ship
Kendall, William, 5, unknown ship

Logan, Sarah, 11, no ship name
Long, John, 5, Blonde, died
Long, Thomas, 9, Blonde
McGuire, David, 13, Jay
McGuire, John, 13, Jay
McNeil, Sam, 16, Christiana
McNight, Hugh, 7, Colin Campbell
McNight, Robert, 11, Colin Campbell, died
Miller, John, 4 mos, June, unknown ship, died
Montgomery, Thomas, 14, Christiana, ret'd to sheds with typhus
O'Brien, George, 9, Manchester
O'Brien, Margaret, 19, Manchester
O'Brien, Mary, 11, Manchester
O'Brien, William, 15, Manchester
Rogers, Ellen, 19, Elizabeth
Scott, Eliza, 13, June, Ship Ajax
Scott, Jane, 11, June, Ship Ajax
Scott, Julia, June, Ship Ajax
Scott, Rebecca, June, Ship Ajax
Scott, Robert, June, Ship Ajax
Scott, Thomas, 8, June, Ship Ajax, died July 20th
Taylor, William, 9, Sarah
Ward, Elizabeth, 14, Lord Seaton
Ward, Emily, 8, unknown ship
Ward, Susan, 7, unknown ship
Watchoram/Watchhorn, Dora, 18, Pandora
Watchoram/Watchhorn, Eliza, 12, Pandora
Watchoram/Watchhorn, Rebecca, 24, Pandora
Watchorn, Robert, 14, Pandora
Wells, Sarah, 16, John Bolton

Total 54 orphans, 10 deaths, 44 living

Part of note attached reads "*It will be noticed that among the Girls many are of an age which at first sight might be deemed inadmissible to an Orphan Asylum, but in fact they are all greater objects of compassion than the very young children from their state of debility and utter helplessness.*"

See images at
http://www.olivetreegenealogy.com/Ebooks/Orphans1847/

Passenger Books of J & J Cooke 1847-1871

J & J Cooke were Shipping Agents with sailings from Londonderry Ireland to Quebec and St. John New Brunswick from 1847 to 1871. Luckily the company kept its shipping records and thus the names of Irish passengers on board these ships have survived.

You can view the lists of names of passengers at http://www.olivetreegenealogy.com/ships/jjcooke.shtml

Fitzwilliam Estate Immigrants 1847-1855

In the late 1840s a program of assisted emigration was initiated by Lord Fitzwilliam to reduce the number of tenants on his estate in southwest County Wicklow Ireland.

Most of these emigrants sailed from New Ross to Quebec City, but few of them stayed in Quebec, where the population was for the most part French-speaking. Instead, they continued on up the St. Lawrence River to the province of Ontario (then called Upper Canada) and became part of Irish communities there.

The online database lists many of the Irish from the Fitzwilliam estate who settled in the West 1/2 of Ontario, from roughly Belleville to Lake Huron. To view the lists, see

http://www.ancestorsatrest.com/ireland_genealogy_data/wicklow_ontario_fitzwilliam_estate.shtml

Emigration Agent Returns of Emigrant Orphans, 1847

These lists are from the 1847 Records of Emigrant Agent A.J. Buchanan. They consist of

- Semi-monthly return of Roman Catholic orphan children in charge of the archbishop of Quebec
- Names of orphan children entrusted to the care of the Ladies of the good Pastor, Montreal
- Names of orphan children in charge of the Bishop of Montreal
- List of orphans given in charge and disposed of by the Archbishop of Quebec
- List of orphans sent to and given by the Rev. P. McMahon
- Return of orphan children in charge of the Montreal Protestant Orphan Asylum
- Semi-monthly return of orphan children in charge of the Bishop of Montreal

(Pay to view) Consult
http://search.ancestry.ca/search/db.aspx?dbid=1553

New York Almshouse Inmates in 1850-1855 who first arrived in Canada

This database contains the extracted names of inmates in the New York Almshouse who arrived in Canada before going on to New York.

In the early 1800's port cities in the USA bore the burden of immigration. By the time they arrived, so many immigrants were tired, hungry and poor they ended up in the City Almshouse. This meant the citizens had to take care of them. At first the citizens of the city asked the Mayors for funds to support the poor. Eventually they asked the states, and by mid-century some states (PA, NY, MA) set up State agencies to deal with the issue. Eventually, beginning in the 1880's, the Federal Government nationalized the programs.

Dating back to the colonial era, New York City assumed responsibility for its citizens who were destitute, sick, homeless, or otherwise unable to care for themselves. The city maintained an almshouse, various hospitals, and a workhouse on Blackwell's Island (now called Roosevelt Island) for the poor.

There are 2 pages for each name in the original ledger. Information includes Individual's name, age, where they are from (Nativity), Name of Ship, Date of sailing, Ports of departure and arrival, Captain's Name, Owner's Name, Date of Bond, Sureties, Date Discharged, Death Date and Remarks.

This free database may be viewed at

http://www.rootsweb.com/~ote/ships/ny_alms1855.htm

Kingston Ontario Arrivals 1861-1882

This is a Return of Emigrants Landed at the Port of Kingston Ontario, Canada 1861-1882. It gives the final destination of the individuals, their date of arrival at Kingston and more.

Details provided for each individual are Date of Landing; Name of Emigrant or Head of Family; From what Country; Via what Seaport Town; Destination; Condition, general appearance, health; No. of male adults; No. of Female adults; No. under 6 years; No. over 6 years and under 12; in what Township Employed as Servants; In what Township settled, or bought land; Amount of passage tickets issued; Amount of provisions; Amount of Medical aid; amount of Capital brought by them; General Remarks.

See http://olivetreegenealogy.com/ships/kingston1861oct-1862may.shtml

Index to Miscellaneous Immigrants to Canada Before 1865

A number of lists have been indexed by name in this database. Many of the records relate to immigrants from the British Isles to Quebec and Ontario, but there are also references to settlers in other provinces. The database also includes other types of records such as declarations of aliens and names of some Irish orphans.

View the records at http://www.bac-lac.gc.ca/eng/discover/immigration/immigration-records/immigrants-before-1865/Pages/introduction.aspx

Colonial Archives Database

This online database contains over 70,000 detailed descriptions of documents in the archival collection mainly of the British and French colonial periods. The dates covered are

- French Regime (1608-1760)
- British Regime (1760-1865)

Use the French keyword "passagers" to view the 526 entries re passengers to New France (present day Quebec) and other locations. Note that the records are NOT duplicated in both English & French. For example "passengers" gives 89 hits only

To search the online database, consult
http://www.collectionscanada.gc.ca/archivianet/020112_e.html

Made in the USA
Middletown, DE
15 April 2019